Summer Jobs and Opportunities for Teenagers

Molly Delano

A LifeWorks® Guide

PERSEUS
PUBLISHING
A Member of the Perseus Books Group

Library of Congress Control Number: 2003100273
ISBN 0-7382-0896-5

Perseus Publishing is a Member of the Perseus Books Group.
Find us on the World Wide Web at http://www.perseuspublishing.com.

Perseus Publishing books are available at special discounts for bulk purchases in the U.S. by corporations, institutions, and other organizations. For more information, please contact the Special Markets Department at the Perseus Books Group, 11 Cambridge Center, Cambridge, MA 02142, or call (800) 255–1514 or (617) 252–5298, or e-mail j.mccrary@perseusbooks.com

1 2 3 4 5 6 7 8 9 10—06 05 04 03

Contents

A summer job can bring you lots of things: experience, new friends, fun, and—of course—money. An internship or volunteer opportunity may give you insight into a particular career plus the chance to grow and learn. But how do you know what kind of job to get? How do you apply?

This book will answer these questions and more, taking you through the job search process step by step, from figuring out what you want to do, to finding and applying for a position, to managing your money and learning about taxes. And you can use the resource list of related Web sites and books as a guide for researching summer opportunities and getting more information.

Planning your summer

Summer jobs and opportunities are a great way to investigate a field you're interested in. For example, if you've thought about becoming a teacher, a job as a camp counselor, child care worker, or full-time baby-sitter would be an easy way to find out if you really do like that kind of work.

You can also take a summer job and turn it into the kind of experience a future employer—or college admissions officer—might be impressed by. If you have plans to get a job as a union laborer when you graduate, a summer job as an apprentice might make it possible for you to start working at higher pay in the future. Or, if you are thinking about majoring in nursing, summer employment in an assisted-living facility would show an admissions officer that you're serious about your career.

Maybe you're just interested in having some extra money in your pocket and meeting new people. Getting a job as a lifeguard at a local pool, as a clerk in a music store, or as a waiter could be just the opportunity you're looking for.

"Tonight Show" host Jay Leno started off his career working as a "lot boy" during the summer, cleaning and washing cars at a Ford dealership near his home in Andover, Massachusetts.

There are other benefits to a summer job besides a paycheck and work experience, including

- the chance to learn something new

- a boost in self-confidence

- a new sense of independence

- the ability to work as part of a team

The right job can give you all of these things. But finding the right job isn't always easy. That's why it's important to start early and think hard about what you want out of your summer.

Thinking ahead

Before you begin to think about possible jobs and opportunities, you need to have a realistic understanding of what you can do in terms of your schedule and your individual needs. You should also take the time to talk to your parents or other adults in your home. They may be able to help you set some guidelines about the kind of schedule you can work and how much money you need to make. Here are some general questions you should think about:

- What kind of hours do you want to work? Full time? Part time?

- Is there a minimum amount of money you need to save for next year?

- Are you planning to take a vacation with your family this summer?

- When does school get out? When does it start again?

- Do you want to work in the morning or at night?

- How will you get to a job?

- Are there physical limitations to what you can do?

When you have the answers to these questions like these, you'll know what you have to work with. For example, if you need to save $2,000 to pay for gas and car insurance during the school year, then you'll need to make sure you get a job that will pay at least that. Or maybe you'll decide you want your days free this summer, so a night job like washing dishes in a restaurant or collecting tickets at a movie theater would be right for you.

Once you decide on the basic parameters—finances, general schedule, when you can work and when you can't—you can start looking at different job possibilities.

One important note about summer jobs: you need to start looking early. Many popular jobs are filled as early as April. In order to start off with a full range of options, it's good to begin planning your summer in February or March. Unless you know exactly what you want to do, it may take a few weeks just to zero in on the right opportunity, and then another few weeks to get all the details lined up.

When you're thinking about your ideal summer opportunity, consider the realities of holding down a job. You'll have to show up on time, dress appropriately, honor commitments, possibly skip other activities for work, and answer to a manager. While it might seem that these requirements are obvious, it's important to be mentally prepared to make some sacrifices for work. But the return on those sacrifices can be huge—money, experience, and the opportunity to learn something new.

"When my parents told me that I needed to get a job last summer, I had no idea what I wanted to do. I didn't think I was even qualified for anything except playing video games. But I called up a local software company and got a really cool programming job in their office that paid a ton of money."

— Jennifer, 17

What's right for you?

The "classic" summer jobs for teenagers are at places like amusement parks, restaurants, and movie theaters. But you can also work in a factory, office, store, camp, national park, nursing home, or library. You can deal with people all day long or have no personal interaction at all. Because the range of possibilities is so large, you might want to start by looking at some of the basic job types that exist.

There are people-oriented jobs like

- camp counselor

- clothing store employee

- coffee shop employee

- music store employee

- babysitter

And there are skill-oriented jobs like

- construction worker

- landscaper

- computer technician

- painter

- lifeguard

Inventor Thomas Edison's first job was as a newspaper and candy vendor for a railroad line in Michigan.

Figuring out what you're good at

Even if you've never had a job before, you have skills that an employer would consider valuable. It's just a matter of figuring out exactly what those skills are. Things you do every day in school or at home are transferable to a job.

Maybe you're great in math—an asset that would serve you well in a cashier position. If you're great with kids, that's a skill you could put to use as a camp counselor or babysitter. Are you athletic? Consider a job as a lifeguard or as a sports instructor at a summer day or overnight camp. Ask your friends or family members what they think you're good at if you need some help getting started.

Another way of starting your job search is by focusing on your interests. Your interests—the things you do with your friends or whenever you have free time—actually help you develop skills that can be applied to any job. Are you a sports fiend? Why not look for a job at a stadium taking tickets or selling refreshments? If you're interested in art, check out galleries, art supply stores, art camps, and museums to see what they offer in the way of summer employment.

You can also get some ideas about potential jobs by thinking about what you're good at and what interests you at school. If you're an English or history whiz, you might be a good reader and writer, and enjoy interacting with other people. Here are some job ideas for you:

- bookstore clerk

- library assistant

- intern at a magazine or newspaper

- tutor

- administrative assistant

If you're better at science or biology classes, think about jobs like

- laboratory assistant

- nurse's aide

- landscaper

- employee at a garden center or plant store

- groundskeeper

Is math or computer science your specialty? Consider a job like

- cashier

- bank teller

- computer support technician

- computer programmer

- data processor

- employee at a computer or appliance store

If you're interested in music or the arts, think about jobs like

- movie theater employee

- art store employee

- children's art or music instructor

- painter

- tour guide at a museum

If you excel in technical subjects or physical activities, consider jobs like

- exercise instructor

- mechanic's assistant

- camp counselor

- construction worker

- carpenter

If you love animals, you might enjoy a job like

- veterinary assistant

- dog walker

- pet groomer

- pet store clerk

- zoo employee

"I've always been really into music, so I got a job at a music store in the mall. I get to listen to all the new releases as soon as they come out and I also get a discount."

— Juan, 15

Outdoor jobs

Thousands of teenagers work in summer camps and national parks each summer. If you love the outdoors, this could be a great way to earn money and possibly explore another part of the country. If you think you might be interested in working at a camp or national park, be sure you apply early—that may mean as soon as March—because these are popular jobs that fill up rapidly each spring.

Working for the National Park Service is almost a rite of passage for many American teenagers. Each year thousands of high school and college students take summer jobs at big parks like the Grand Canyon or Yellowstone, or at the National Park Service's nearly 400 other parks. The National Park Service is run by the U.S. Department of the Interior, which sometimes hires employees directly. Otherwise, the parks themselves do the hiring. For summer jobs at state parks, you can check with your state park organization.

The types of jobs you can have at national and state parks vary widely. They include

- rangers

- fee collectors

- groundskeepers

- housekeepers

- cooks

- tour guides

- laborers

- carpenters

- cashiers

- clerks

It's important to remember that not all park jobs are in the outdoors. Large parks need staff members to run hotels, restaurants, and equipment rental and gift shops as well as to mow lawns and collect tickets.

If you're interested in exploring a new part of the country, a national park job may be able to provide you with this experience as well as a paycheck. Some jobs also provide housing for summer employees, which can be a great way to make new friends. To find out more, check the resource list at the end of this book.

Other places to look for outdoor jobs include golf courses, local beaches or pools, amusement parks, landscaping companies, or community recreation programs that hire instructors to teach swimming, basketball, or other activities.

Amusement parks are another place many teenagers turn to for summer jobs. If you have an amusement park in your community, you could get a job taking tickets, running games, managing lines, serving food, working in a gift shop, or working on a cleanup crew. If there's not a big park near you, check out local miniature golf course, go-kart tracks, or skating rinks.

Before he traveled through space, astronaut John Glenn paid his dues as a kitchen worker at a YMCA summer camp in Ohio.

Summer camps

Summer camps cater to a wide variety of interests. There are adventure camps, music camps, computer camps, craft camps, day camps, sleepover camps, and even astronaut camps. And they all need counselors, cooks, dishwashers, instructors, and groundskeepers. These positions, especially counselors or counselors-in-training (CITs) are almost exclusively teenagers.

Though counselor jobs don't usually pay extravagantly, they do usually offer free housing and food, as well as countless opportunities for developing leadership skills. Counselors usually instruct campers, supervise entertainment and activities, resolve conflicts, comfort lonely or sad kids, and act as round-the-clock leaders for a group of campers.

Many camps hire CITs who attended the camp in the past because they are familiar with the organization and how it works. If you attended a camp when you were younger, you may want to contact that organization about counselor positions.

As a general rule, counselors must be motivated and good at motivating others. A good counselor is also mature, patient, creative, and flexible. You can check the resource list at the end of this book for more information about camp counselor jobs.

Working for yourself

Some teenagers have a particular skill that lends itself to self-employment. Some teenagers have started up formal businesses like Web site design companies, while others have decided to work for themselves on a more casual basis by, babysitting, walking pets, or cleaning houses.

Starting up a business is an excellent crash course in both economics and independence, but it can also be really hard work. If you're thinking of working for yourself, make sure you talk to a parent or professional to figure out if you'll be able to earn enough money, how you'll attract clients, and what kinds of taxes you might have to pay.

Some self-employed teenagers have been incredibly successful, but they worked a lot of long, hard hours building their businesses from the ground up. If your summer objective is to earn some money and meet new people, this might not be the best route for you. But if you've got a skill or idea that you're burning to sell and you're willing to do what it takes, then starting up your own business could be the perfect solution.

Here are ways teenagers can earn money on their own:

- mowing lawns

- babysitting

- dog walking

- house sitting

- selling crafts or baked goods

- designing Web sites

- cleaning houses or offices

- washing cars

Actress Jennifer Love Hewitt got her start by singing at county fairs and livestock shows near her hometown of Killeen, Texas.

What's it really all about?

Once you've narrowed down your list of possible jobs
to a handful, it's time to enlist the help of friends and
family to figure out what each job would really entail. A
nine-dollar-an-hour job on an assembly line may sound
great, but what would it really be like? In order to make
an informed decision about what you're going to do this
summer, you'll need to do some investigating. Ask your
parents and friends if they know anyone who has
worked at a factory or on an assembly line. Then find
out what it's really like. Ask what a typical day on the
job is like, about the dynamics between management
and employees, whether or not there is flexibility with
schedules and hours, and whether there are opportunities to socialize.

"Last summer I got a job as a dishwasher at a
restaurant. I thought I'd be able to just do my
thing without people bothering me, but it turned
out to be really stressful because the
restaurant was so busy. Next time I'll definitely
work someplace more relaxed."

— Andy, 16

These information-gathering questions may bring to light some issues that you weren't aware of. For example, if you are thinking of getting a factory job and talk to your uncle who has worked in factories all his life, he might tell you that the job pays well, but most of the employees are likely to be much older than you and there's not much chance to socialize. If your priorities include making new friends and having fun, you may want to look elsewhere.

Finding and
applying for a job

Your community may have dozens of organizations that help teenagers find summer work. There are national agencies, like the United Way, as well as local community development agencies that can be excellent resources. Your school guidance office is a good place to look for help locating and contacting these organizations. It's important to remember that programs like these often start placing teenagers in summer jobs as early as March or April, so it's a good idea to investigate these options as soon as possible. Your guidance office may also be a clearinghouse for jobs with your community's park and recreation departments as well as local businesses looking for summer help.

Networking

You may have heard the word "networking" before. Though it's usually used in a business setting, networking—reaching out to friends, family, and acquaintances for help with your job search—can be a really useful tool.

Once you have a general idea of what you want to do, talk to your parents, your friends, your friends' parents, and all of your relatives and acquaintances. People don't have to be business experts to have a connection that could be helpful to you. Maybe your aunt knows someone who manages a restaurant you'd like to work at or your mother's company is hiring summer interns for filing or data processing. You don't have to call up strangers when you're networking—it's just a matter of talking to the people you already know and telling them about your job search.

Other ways to find a job

You can also talk to teachers, guidance counselors, coaches, and fellow members of a religious or social community. You never know who might turn up a great opportunity.

There are other ways to look for jobs. You can scan the Help Wanted ads in your local newspaper, but keep in mind that many of these businesses may be looking to hire help immediately, not three or four months from now. You can still contact a business that interests you and ask if they will be hiring any summer help. It never hurts to be ahead of the crowd when it comes to looking for a job.

The most direct route for securing a summer job is to identify where you want to work and then simply walk in and ask if they hire summer employees. This is probably the best approach for traditional summer jobs like retail sales, restaurant work, or child care. If you decide to use this approach, don't forget to have an up-to-date resume and references on hand and wear appropriate clothing. Walk in prepared to be inter-viewed. You should also be sure to follow up each contact with a potential employer with a thank you letter or phone call.

When you're looking for a job you can also check online employment sites (see the resource list at the end of this book), look in the Yellow Pages to pinpoint specific stores or companies, read the classified ads in your local paper, and look for Help Wanted signs at stores and other places of business.

Here are some more places to look for a summer job:

- your favorite stores

- local hotels or resorts

- tourist attractions

- local corporations

- fast food and other restaurants

- places that need delivery services (newspapers, dry cleaners, or restaurants)

Automotive pioneer Henry Ford's first job was as a machine shop apprentice. He also worked as a watch repairman at night.

Filling out an application

It's important to be ready to be interviewed when you go to fill out an application for a job. Many employers like to interview people on the spot instead of scheduling an appointment for several days later.

This means that you have to look and be prepared. For more information about interviews, read the section on page 47.

As you're filling out applications, you may be tempted to leave a section blank because you're not sure what it's asking for or to "fudge" a little on a previous job or experience. Don't do it. It's easy for employers to check up on the information you put on your application, and many do.

Employers also prefer to see complete applications. If you leave a section blank, your application may get overlooked. If you don't understand something on the application, bring it home and ask a relative or teacher for help, or ask the employer to clarify the instructions.

Try to remember that just as you'll be checking out a potential job site and employer when you pick up an application, he or she will be forming a first impression of you. That's why it's important to wear appropriate clothes and be prepared with everything you'll need to fill out the application. Here are some tips:

- Dress conservatively. You have to wear a dress or a suit, but you should look clean and put together. This means no torn t-shirts or jeans, sunglasses, or hats. By dressing appropriately, you'll be telling your potential employer that you want the job and you care about making a good first impression.

- Bring your own pen. Never ask if you can borrow a pen. This could send a signal that you're not serious about applying for the job.

- Be prepared to talk about when you can start, what days and hours you're available for work, and your past work experience. Have a resume (turn to the next page for help writing a resume) or at least a list of references, including telephone numbers.

- If a parent or friend is with you, ask them to wait outside to show employers that you can do things on your own.

Creating a resume

A resume might seem like a waste of time for someone who doesn't have a work history, but presenting a resume to a potential employer is a way of saying that you're serious about employment, which may set you apart from other applicants. Resumes are also important for people applying for jobs or volunteer opportunities so far from home that a personal interview is impractical.

Think of your resume as an advertisement for you. It should include these key pieces of information:

- contact information

- experience

- summary of skills and qualifications

- education

The "Experience" section of your resume doesn't have to be blank if you've never had a job. It can include classes you've taken that might be relevant to the job you're applying for. For example, if you're applying for a job as a mechanic's assistant and you've taken several advanced shop classes, this would be the section you would use to highlight that experience.

"The first time I tried to write a resume I had no idea what to put down. I'd never even had a job except for mowing lawns. But I asked my guidance counselor for help and she told me about some Web sites and books that explain the whole thing. It's not too hard once you've figured out what to do."

— Chris, 15

This section can also include activities and interests that may be relevant to the job you're applying for. If one of your hobbies is Web site design and you created sites for friends or relatives, mention that here. If you're applying for a position as a child care provider and most of your experience comes from the fact that you're the oldest of six children, that's something an employer should know about.

When you're brainstorming about your experience, try to remember that practically everything you do or have done has some value and can be turned into relevant experience. Were you in charge of running a school event? Are you the captain of a sports team? Did you volunteer at a senior center? Those three activities alone show initiative, leadership, and organizational skills.

References

References are the names and phone numbers of adults who know you well and are aware of your capabilities. References don't necessarily have to be past employers, but you shouldn't use family members or friends. If you don't have a past employer to use as a reference, you may want to consider asking a

- family friend

- teacher

- coach

- guidance counselor

- neighbor

- religious leader

Two references are usually enough. You can list their names at the bottom of your resume or you can provide them when and if an employer asks for them. Always remember to let your references know if they might be getting a call about you. Most people—even people who are close to you—don't like being put on the spot without warning.

All of this information should be collected into a neat, professional-looking format that can be easily read—no spelling or grammar mistakes. You can use the sample resumes on pages 42-43 as a guide for creating your own.

"I put a teacher down as a reference but I forgot to tell her. When they called and asked her about me they used my real name instead of my nickname. She told them that she had never heard of me. She felt bad when she realized what happened, but it was too late."

— Matt, 15

Cover letters

If a resume is a summary of who you are and what you can do, a cover letter is an introduction. You may not need a cover letter if you are planning to walk into a store and ask for a job, but if you apply for a job through the mail, you'll need to write a cover letter to accompany your resume.

Cover letters don't have to be long—an employer just wants a clear, concise description of what job you are applying for and why she should consider you as a candidate. Every letter should end with information about how to reach you and a thank you.

Good cover letters don't pretend to be something they aren't. It's not necessary to write a very formal, long letter. You can let your personality come through, but make sure you triple check any letter for spelling or grammar mistakes.

Take a look at the sample cover letter on page 45 for some ideas about what a cover letter should say and what it should look like.

Tammy Davis
1904 Circle Park Rd.
Los Angeles, CA 10001
(555) 555-5555

EXPERIENCE

6/01-8/01	Fun World Theme Park. Cashier at park. Responsible for opening and closing registers, handling money, and interacting with visitors.
7/00-8/00	Ice Cream Dream. Counter person. Responsible for serving customers, opening and closing registers, handling money.
9/00-Present	Donald Williams. Babysitter for 6-year-old child on regular basis.
EDUCATION	Currently a junior at Bayside High School.
INTERESTS	Music, hiking, biking, and other outdoor activities.

Carlos Sanchez
1334 Twenty Eighth Street #5
Watertown, NY 12345
(517) 622-9987
carlos@email.com

JOB OBJECTIVE: Counselor-in-training position

QUALIFICATIONS:

- Excellent swimmer

- Good at communicating with children

- Experienced camper

- Certified lifeguard with CPR training

EXPERIENCE:

- Volunteer tennis and swimming instructor at local YMCA

- Two years of babysitting experience

WORK HISTORY:

- Counselor, Watertown YMCA day camp, summer 2001

EDUCATION:

- Sophomore, Watertown High School, Watertown, NY

REFERENCES:

- Paul Jones, Swim Coach, Watertown High School. (517) 456-7890

- Maria Lopez, Camp Director, Watertown YMCA. (517) 789-1000

Carlos Sanchez
1334 Twenty Eighth Street #5
Watertown, NY 12345
(517) 622-9987
carlos@email.com

March 25, XXXX

Mr. Mark Smith
Camp High Meadow
123 Allen Street
Watertown, NY 12345

Dear Mr. Smith,

I am an experienced athletic instructor with a special interest in teaching children. I would like to apply for a counselor-in-training position at Camp High Meadow for the summer of XXXX.

Because I was a camper myself for several summers, I am familiar with many of the duties and responsibilities that a CIT must undertake. I believe my experience instructing children at the summer day camp at the Watertown YMCA last year has prepared me to take on the challenge of a CIT position at Camp High Meadow.

At the Anytown YMCA, I led arts and crafts activities and organized sports and other recreational activities for more than 20 children between the ages of 7 and 12. I also worked with the Camp Director to make schedules and plan new programs.

I enjoy working with children, and my creativity, flexibility, and leadership skills would make me a great CIT. I would like to talk to you about working at Camp High Meadow. I will call you within the week to set up a time for an interview. Thank you for taking the time to look at my resume and for considering my qualifications.

Sincerely,

Carlos Sanchez

Interviewing

Not all jobs that you apply for will require an interview, but if you do have to have one, it's important to keep one key piece of information in mind: An interview is a two-way process. It's a chance for both you and your potential employer to figure out if you're the right person for the job, and the only way to find out is for both of you to ask questions.

An interview is a short meeting, usually 15 or 20 minutes, during which the employer will ask you questions. Before you go to an interview, look the following questions over and think about what you might say. You don't have to have a completely prepared answer, but you should have a basic idea of how you would respond to any of these questions:

- Why do you want this job?

- Do you have any experience?

- Why would you be good at this job?

- What hours and days are you available to work?

- How much money do you expect to make?

- How do you handle disagreements with others?

- What would you do if . . . You saw someone stealing? Your friends asked you to give them something without paying? You had plans to go away for the weekend and then you found out you were scheduled to work?

The most important thing you can do during an interview is be yourself—as long as you are polite and honest. And remember, it's fine to take a moment to organize your thoughts before answering a question.

It's also important to

- Be on time—or even a few minutes early

- Dress appropriately

- Don't chew gum

- Bring a pen

- Smile

- Shake hands with the interviewer and address her by name

- Make eye contact with the interviewer throughout the interview

- Bring several copies of your resume and the names and phone numbers of at least two references

At the end of the interview, the interviewer may ask if you have any questions. Here are some that you may want to ask:

- What would my specific duties be if I worked here?

- Who would I report to?

- Is there a dress code or uniform?

- If I need to take time off, will that be OK?

- How many hours and days would I be working?

- Would I be trained?

- What is the rate of pay? Will I be eligible for pay increases?

When the interview has been completed, shake the interviewer's hand and thank him for his time. You can also ask, "When will you be making a decision?" or something along those lines so you will know when you will be notified about the job. If you haven't heard back within the stated period of time, call back and ask to speak with the person who interviewed you. You could say something like, "Hi, my name is Tammy and I interviewed with you last week. I was wondering if you have selected someone for the job we talked about."

Rebecca Lobo, star basketball player in the WNBA, worked as a tobacco picker for five summers on a farm in Massachusetts.

You may also want to send a thank you letter to the interviewer. This is not necessary for all job interviews, but if there is a lot of competition for the position or you want to really make a good impression, a thank you note can be a great tool.

Here's an example of a thank you letter:

Carlos Sanchez
1334 Twenty Eighth Street #5
Watertown, NY 12345
(517) 622-9987

March 12, 2002

Mark Smith
Camp High Meadow
123 Allen Street
Watertown, NY 12345

Dear Mr. Smith,

Thank you for taking the time to talk with me last week. I am still very interested in the counselor-in-training position at Camp High Meadow and I hope that you will consider me for the job. I look forward to hearing from you.

Sincerely,

Carlos Sanchez

Internships and volunteer opportunities

Internships and volunteer opportunities are great ways to get involved in an issue or field you want to know more about. An internship is the same as a job, but it's not always a paid position. Internships are available in every field and career possible—and if they don't exist, it's possible to create an internship or volunteer opportunity.

Interns and volunteers work in Congress, in Hollywood, for non-profit environmental agencies, for community-based groups, and at museums, hospitals, and local government agencies. While internships and volunteer opportunities may not pay much—or anything—the benefits you reap can be invaluable.

Internships and volunteer opportunities can also provide experience that helps when you apply to future jobs or for college. Students who pursue internships and opportunities in the fields they are interested in show initiative and dedication, two things employers and college admissions officers value in a candidate.

"Last summer I worked as an intern at a radio station. It was really cool. I got to sit in with the DJs while they were on the air, help them make song lists, and go to advertising and marketing meetings. Plus I got class credit for it."

— Maria, 16

Internships

There are many different kinds of internships: unpaid, paid, full time, part time, and ones that could pay off with course credit. The key point of an internship is that it provides you with experience of some kind. You can become an intern in an established program, maybe at the place where one of your parents or another relative works, or you can develop your own internship opportunity and try to find someone to hire you.

There are lots of potential benefits to internships, including

- school credit (check with your guidance office)

- work experiences you may not get through a regular paying job

- an inside view of a particular career or organization

- references for future jobs or personal recommendations for college applications

The process of developing your own internship is a lot like finding the right job. You have to start off with some brainstorming about your interests, goals, and abilities. You might begin by thinking about the benefits of an internship instead of a paid job, and then consider which option is best for you. Then think about what field you want to gain experience in and where in your community you could get that experience.

The exciting thing about internships is that the possibilities are limitless—but that can also make it hard to pin down exactly what kind of internship you want. If you're interested in music, check with local radio stations, concert promoters, or theaters to see if they have internships or would be willing to take on an intern. If you're interested in writing, look into interning at a local newspaper or magazine. If math or science is your strong suit, you could intern at a hospital or a high-tech company.

When you establish an internship, make sure that both you and your employer or sponsor are clear about what your responsibilities are and to whom you will be reporting.

Talk to your parents, relatives, and family friends about their jobs and whether their places of employment offer summer internships. They can tell you about possible opportunities and put you in touch with the people who run the program.

For more ideas about internships and how to find or create one, check the resource list at the end of this book.

"I've always loved animals, and I really wanted to work with them last summer, so I called up the zoo in my city and talked to the director. They didn't have any paying jobs, but we worked out an internship that let me work actually taking care of the animals every week. I didn't make any money, but they told me that when I come back this year I'll be a paid employee."

— Sarah, 15

Volunteering

Volunteers are basically unpaid workers who do a job because it's in a field or for an organization they have a strong interest in. If you are thinking about volunteering this summer, make sure that earning money isn't a priority for you—volunteers work out of the kindness of their hearts, not to fill up their bank accounts. But volunteer positions do sometimes turn into paid jobs in the future, after you've proven yourself to be a valuable member of the organization.

Hospitals, animal shelters, schools, museums, zoos, environmental groups, community centers, political action groups, and organizations that serve older people all rely on volunteers. They ask volunteers to donate time, skills, talents, and even just plain old enthusiasm to reach their goals.

Volunteer positions provide many of the same benefits that internships do. They can offer insight into a particular field or organization that may help when you're thinking about careers or applying for college. But volunteer positions can do much more than provide experience or an extra line on your resume. They may give you an opportunity to feel great about yourself while doing something for a larger cause.

"I spend about two hours a week working for a center that helps recent immigrants learn English and find jobs and places to live. I answer the phone and try to help people fill out the paperwork they need. It sounds kind of stupid, but I really do feel like I'm making a difference in their lives."

— Miguel, 15

But be prepared—volunteer jobs, especially those for first-timers—are not usually glamorous. While you can sign up with international or national organizations that place volunteers around the world doing things like environmental research or building houses, most volunteer work is more basic, and involves things like filing, answering telephones, stuffing envelopes, or reading a story to someone who is homebound. If you decide to volunteer this summer, try not to get discouraged if you start to feel like you're not really making a difference. The small contributions of many volunteers really do add up.

Organizations and places that typically rely on volunteers include

- homeless shelters

- food banks

- schools

- state parks

- literacy programs

- hospitals

- libraries

- animal shelters

- senior centers

- environmental organizations

- political campaigns

For more information about volunteer opportunities, check the resource list at the back of this book.

Summer opportunities away from home

Some teenagers travel around the world or across the country for summer jobs. In addition to jobs at summer camps or national parks as ways to investigate other parts of the country, there are plenty of other opportunities to explore places far from home. Teenagers can volunteer to teach English in other countries, participate in wilderness adventures, join an environmental research team on a project overseas, or team up with a community development group doing work in another country.

Many of these opportunities are organized by schools, churches, or community groups. They can be wonderful experiences that help you broaden your horizons and learn about other cultures and ways of life.

If you are thinking about doing an overseas trip this summer, it's important to start planning as early as possible. Many programs fill up quickly because they're so popular. You should also be aware of the potentially high costs of overseas travel. Even though many programs involve volunteering, participants often have to pay for travel and other expenses. Be sure to discuss this with the adults in your family to determine if this is the best choice for you this summer.

You might want to think about financing a more exotic future summer plan by working this summer at a less glamorous job that pays well and saving part of your earnings for the cost.

For more information about summer opportunities overseas or away from home, check the resource list at the end of this book.

"This summer I'm going to travel to Mexico with my church. We're going to help build houses in a small village in the mountains. I'll be gone for two weeks. I can't wait!" — Jamie, 15.

Money and legal matters

If you decide that a paid job is the best plan for you this summer, in addition to deciding how to spend your money, you'll have to think about some other legal and financial issues. These include work permits, taxes, budgeting, and saving.

Earning money can be an exciting feeling. It means that you have more independence and freedom to do the things you want without being dependent on your parents. It also means that you have the freedom to spend all of your hard-earned money buying clothes or CDs. You probably don't want to work all summer only to end up where you started—broke. So it will pay off to take some time to learn how to budget your money, especially if you're saving up to pay for something in particular. You may find that your parents or other adults you know and trust can help you come up with saving and spending guidelines.

Minimum wage

Most teenagers work at jobs that pay *minimum wage,* which is a guideline set by the federal government to help states set their own minimum wage rates or guidelines. Right now, the federal minimum wage is $5.15. But that doesn't mean that the state you live in guarantees that rate to all employees.

States are not required to meet the federal minimum wage rate. In fact, some states have minimum wage rates that are higher than that proposed by the federal government, some states have a minimum wage rate that's lower, and some states don't even have minimum wage laws at all. To find out your state's laws regarding minimum wage, go to the U.S. Department of Labor Web site listed in the resource guide at the end of this book.

Rock legend Elvis Presley once mowed lawns in Memphis, Tennessee, for $4 a yard.

Work permits

Some states have laws about how old people have to be before they can work and what kinds of jobs young people can hold. If you are between 14 and 17, you may need to get a work permit to legally hold a job.

If a work permit is required for a job, your employer should let you know about it when they make you an offer of employment. Work permits are free. If you're a high school student you can probably get a work permit through your school guidance office, but you can also contact your state labor office. To find out how to contact your state labor office, look in the government pages of the phone book or do an Internet search using your state and the words "labor office."

State and federal governments created these labor laws to protect young workers. The government wants to make sure that teenagers aren't overworked and underpaid, so in some cases the laws dictate the number of hours you can work and what kinds of jobs you can do based on your age. The rules vary from state to state, but your school guidance office or state labor office can probably help you understand any restrictions in your state. Federal laws are the same no matter where you live, and they are very specific, especially for people under the age of 18. For example, if you're under 18, you can't

- operate a forklift

- operate many machines, including power saws, meat slicers, or box cutters

- work in a meat packing plant

- work in demolition, mining, logging, excavation, or roofing

- work where explosives are made or stored

If you are 14 or 15, you can't

- bake or cook (except at a serving counter)

- work in warehouses

- do work that involves being on a ladder or scaffolding

- operate power machinery (except for some types of office equipment)

For most 14- and 15-year-olds there are also federal rules about work hours. The maximum number of hours a 14- or 15-year-old can work when school is not in session is 40 hours a week and 8 hours a day.

If you are 14 or 15, don't be discouraged by these laws. They were established with your safety in mind—not to make you unable to work. Many states allow 14- and 15-year-olds to work in agricultural jobs—picking flowers or vegetables or working as farm laborers—and there are plenty of other jobs available to younger teenagers, too.

Taxes and deductions

The first time you look at your paycheck, you may be shocked at the amount of money that you actually end up with. Just because you make $7 an hour doesn't mean that you take home $7 an hour at the end of the week. Taxes take a huge bite out of your earnings, so it's important to figure out what your check is *really* going to look like so you're not surprised. There are several different types of taxes that may be taken out of your check, including

- *Social Security taxes,* which are paid into the Social Security Administration by all working people. The Social Security Administration is a government agency that gives benefits to retired or disabled workers and their families. When you retire or become disabled, you will receive benefits from the Social Security Administration.

- *Medicare taxes,* which are paid into a national health insurance program for people ages 65 and older. Medicare is a government program run much like the Social Security program—people pay into it while they are working and become eligible to receive benefits when they retire or are disabled.

- *State income tax,* which is paid to your state and goes to support programs and initiatives chosen by the state government. The rate of state income tax varies greatly. Some states, like New Hampshire, don't even have an income tax. Your parents, guidance counselor, or employer can tell you what your state's income tax is.

- *Federal income tax* goes to the federal government to support programs and initiatives on a national level.

Your employer pays your taxes for you by taking them directly from your earnings and sending them to the federal and state governments. Unless you have other income during the school year or your witholdings aren't enough, you may only have to fill out some relatively simple tax forms before April 15 of next year.

"I couldn't believe how small my paychecks were after taxes. Practically half my money went to the government. It's not like babysitting when someone just gives you cash or a regular check."

— Laura, 15

To figure out exactly what your check will look like after your taxes are paid, you'll need to determine the difference between *gross income* and *net income*.

- *Gross income* is the amount of money you actually make, whether it is $7 an hour or $50,000 a year.

- *Net income* is the amount of money you take home, also known as *take-home pay*. This is what you have left after all the taxes and other deductions are subtracted from your gross income.

Calculating your paycheck

Use this process to estimate what your net income will actually be.

1. Weekly earnings
Your hourly wage _____ × number
of hours you work each week _____
= weekly earnings   _____

2. Weekly federal income tax
Your weekly earnings multiplied by 15%   _____

3. Weekly Medicare tax
Your weekly earnings multiplied by 1.45%   _____

4. Weekly Social Security tax
Your weekly earnings multiplied by 6.2%   _____

5. Weekly state income tax
Your weekly earnings multiplied by
your state's income tax   _____

6. Total weekly taxes
Add steps 2 through 5   _____

7. Your net weekly income
Subtract weekly taxes from weekly
earnings   _____

Paperwork

On your first day of work you will probably be asked to fill out two forms: an *I-9* and a *W-4*. These forms are relatively simple to complete. Both forms ask for your Social Security number. Social Security numbers are assigned to all U.S. citizens, and are commonly used for identification. Ask your parents or guardian if you have a Social Security number. Many people get them for their children when they are born. If you don't have a number, you will need to get one. You can go to the Social Security Web site, *www.ssa.gov,* to download an application or call the Social Security office (800-772-1213) to have one sent to you. The process may take several weeks, so you should start before you begin applying for jobs. Be sure to bring your Social Security number with you on your first day of work, because you will need it to fill out the *I-9* and *W-4* forms.

"I made awesome money at my waiter job last summer, but I burned right through it buying clothes and CDs. At the end of the summer I barely had anything saved, so the school year wasn't that great. This year I have to try and save something for the rest of the year."
— Marcus, 17

The *W-4* is a tax form that your employer uses to determine how much tax money should be withheld from your paycheck. The form has several questions and lines that you need to fill out, including one that asks if you are single and if you are claimed as a dependent on anyone else's tax forms.

Most teenagers will claim "0" (zero) for this question because they are single and supported by their parents or guardian, who claim them on their own tax form. The *W-4* comes with a worksheet meant to help you understand the questions, but it's always a good idea to bring the form home and ask your parents or another adult to help if you are confused.

The government uses the *I-9* form to be sure you are eligible for employment. To fill out this form you will need several kinds of identification, so bring a license, birth certificate, or passport as well as your Social Security card. There are no questions to answer. You just have to fill in your name and address and your employer will probably make copies of your identification.

Managing your money

Once you start earning a paycheck, you'll need to come up with a plan for how you'll handle your money. Will you open a savings account? A checking account? Will you use a debit card or just an ATM card? And what's the difference between all of these?

Checking and savings accounts are the two main tools people use to manage their money.

A *checking account* is a bank account from which you can write checks. Your money may or may not earn interest depending on the type of account. Some banks have a minimum balance for their checking accounts, which means that you have to have a certain amount of money in your account at all times or you will have to pay a fee.

Most checking—and savings—accounts come with an *ATM (automated teller machine) card.* These plastic cards can be used at ATMs all around the country or even the world. All you need is a PIN (personal identification number), and you can withdraw cash, make deposits, or transfer money from one account to another.

ATM cards are convenient, but there can be some hidden costs to using them because many ATMs charge you a fee. ATMs that are owned by your bank or connected to your bank through an ATM network may be free, but others could charge you $1, $2, or even up to $7 just to use them to access your own account. Find out where you can use your ATM card for free and try to use those whenever possible.

Many checking accounts also include a *debit card,* which is like an ATM card, but you can use it anywhere that a credit card is accepted. This means that when you make purchases with your debit card, the money comes right out of your checking account. Debit cards are very handy—you don't ever have to worry about having cash. But it's also easy to forget that all of those transactions are subtracting money from your account, so it's important to keep track of your debit card purchases and know how much money you have in your account.

A *savings account* is a bank account that earns interest. You can't write checks from a savings account, but you can withdraw money at any time from any ATM machine or at the bank.

If you'll need to pay bills this summer or make other payments, a checking account may be the right choice for you. When you go to the bank to open a checking account, be sure to ask if there are any fees or minimum balances and if they offer any special student accounts.

If you don't need to write checks, a savings account is an easy way to manage your money. You can open a savings account that comes with an ATM card and then just deposit checks and withdraw cash whenever you need to.

Budgeting

Saving money may seem really hard, especially once you actually have some coming in on a regular basis. But saving and budgeting are two important life skills that will save you a lot of time and frustration if you learn them now.

In order to save money—or at least to avoid spending everything you earn—you'll need to be able to honestly differentiate between what you *need* and what you *want*. This can be hard, especially if you're earning money for the first time.

But budgeting is essential, particularly if you need to pay for things like clothes, books, or entertainment later on during the school year when those weekly paychecks from a summer job are just a memory.

Creating a budget is actually easy—sticking to it is the hard part. The first step is thinking about your financial goals. For some people, this might be being able to pay for going out to the movies on the weekends, while for others, saving money for college may be the biggest priority.

Once you know what you're working for, it's important to think about how much you need to save as well as how much you make and how much you spend. One of the best ways to track your spending is to record all of the money you spend in a week. This includes the pack of gum at the convenience store, new CDs, clothes, magazines, gas money, and subway tokens. Try keeping track of your expenses for one week to see where your money goes. Write down everything that you spend money on in a journal. You might be surprised at how quickly those little purchases add up.

Once you've seen where your money really goes, unless you're a very careful spender, it's probably time to think about where you can cut back on your expenses. One rule of thumb is to always wait a few weeks before buying something that you don't need. For example, if there's a new CD you've been desperate to buy, force yourself to wait two weeks—maybe by that time you won't be interested any more.

If you look carefully at your expenses journal, you may be able to see patterns. Do you spend a lot of money on magazines? Food? Candy? The movies? If there's one thing you tend to go overboard on, ask yourself if it's something you can live without. If it is, then cut back on your spending.

Making a budget

Budgeting isn't as complicated as it sounds—you just need to spend less than you make. But it's easier said than done. You don't have to be vigilant about tracking every expense or constantly worry about spending your money when you're trying to save it. If there's a certain amount of money you need to save by the end of the summer, you have the perfect starting point for a budget.

For example, if you need to save $500 to put into your college savings by the end of the summer, all you need to do is figure out exactly how much you have to put aside from each paycheck. If your net weekly earnings are $125 and you're planning on working for eight weeks, you'll need to set aside $62.50 each week to reach your $500 total by the end of the summer.

Actually setting the money aside can be hard. Here are some ideas for making sure you really save the amount that you need:

- *Deposit the portion of your check that you want to save into a savings account at the same time you cash or deposit your check.* Getting in the habit of separating money that you want to save and money that it's OK to spend is a great way to save.

- *Ask your parents or a relative to keep your savings in a separate account.* This is a good strategy for teenagers who don't have their own checking accounts. You can give the money that you want to save to a trusted family member for safekeeping.

- *Open checking and savings accounts and ask the bank to automatically take money out of your checking and deposit it into your savings on a regular basis.* This way you won't have to do anything—the bank will make your deposits for you. But you have to make sure the money is actually there so it can be withdrawn and deposited into a savings account.

If you're more worried about not spending all of your money than you are about saving a certain amount, you need to be careful about tracking your expenses. If you regularly compare your spending to your earnings, you'll know when the two are out of balance.

A foot in the door

Finding the summer job that's right for you isn't always easy. You need to think about what you want to do and what you need to do, and try to choose a job that meets both descriptions. You can use this book as guide to the entire process, from choosing a job to managing your paycheck. It's also a good idea to talk with your parents, relatives, teachers, or guidance counselors. They may suggest ideas you haven't thought of and they can probably help you think about the kinds of jobs you're best suited for.

The most important thing you can do is start early. If you take the time to think hard about your options and goals, you're likely to end up with a job that makes you happy, meets your needs, and serves as a satisfying gateway to the world of work.

Helpful Web sites
and books

The following list of Web sites and books can help you figure out what kind of job you want, how to apply, and where to look for great opportunities.

General job information

Wet Feet
www.wetfeet.com

Summer Jobs
www.summerjobs.com

Cool Works
www.coolworks.com

Peterson's
www.Petersons.com

Fun Jobs
www.funjobs.com

Monster
www.monstertrak.com

JobGusher
www.jobgusher.com

Teens4Hire.com
www.teens4hire.com

Snag A Job
qwww.snagajob.com

Aboutjobs.com
www.aboutjobs.com

StudentJobs.gov
www.studentjobs.gov

Intern Jobs
www.internjobs.com

Job Monkey
www.jobmonkey.com

Summer Camp Staff
www.summercampstaff.com

Quintessential Careers
www.quintcareers.com

The Teenager's Guide to the Real World Online!
www.bygpub.com/books/tg2rw/summerjobs.htm

Outdoor and volunteer opportunities

My Summers
www.mysummers.com

Earthwatch
www.earthwatch.com

Council Exchanges
www.councilexchanges.com

Global Routes
www.globalroutes.org

Amigos de las Americas
www.amigoslink.org

Volunteers for Peace
www.vfp.org

Volunteermatch
www.volunteermatch.org

Habitat for Humanity
www.habitat.org

City Year
www.cityyear.org

Camp Jobs
www.campjobs.com

Back Door Jobs
www.backdoorjobs.com

Life Guarding Jobs
www.lifeguardingjobs.com

Seasonal Jobs
www.seasonaljobs.net

Resort Jobs
www.resortjobs.com

Legal and financial information

Taxi, the Internal Revenue Service's online magazine
for kids
www.irs.gov/taxi

U.S. Department of Labor
www.dol.gov

Resumes and cover letters

Damn Good Resume
www.damngood.com

Monster.com
http://content.monster.com/resume

About.com
www.jobsearch.about.com/cs/resumes

Books on summer jobs and internships

Peterson's Summer Jobs USA: Where the Jobs Are & How to Get Them, For Students. (Peterson's Guides)

The Internships Bible, by Mark Oldman. (Princeton Review)

Overseas Summer Jobs. (Peterson's Guides)

Better Than a Lemonade Stand: Small Business Ideas for Kids, by Daryl Berstein. (Words Pub.)

A Teen's Guide to Business: The Secrets to a Successful Enterprise, by Linda Menzies, Oren S. Jenkins, and Rickell Rae Fisher. (Thorndike Press)

50 Great Business Ideas for Teens, by Sarah L. Riehm. (Macmillan)

This guide was created as part of the LifeWorks® employee resource program, a service of Ceridian Corporation. The LifeWorks program offers expert counseling, local and national referrals, and practical information on a wide range of work, personal, and family issues. Until now, LifeWorks publications have been available only to eligible employees or members. Perseus Publishing is making selected LifeWorks publications available to the public in book form for the first time.

Molly Delano is a writer and editor at Ceridian. She has written extensively on parenting topics for the LifeWorks program and writes a monthly newsletter for parents of teenagers. A number of LifeWorks parenting experts contributed to this book.